First Published 2007 by Boxtree
an imprint of Pan Macmillan Ltd
Pan Macmillan, 20 New Wharf Road, London N1 9RR
Basingstoke and Oxford
Associated companies throughout the world
www.panmacmillan.com

ISBN 978-0-7522-2659-0

9 8 7 6 5 4 3 2

A CIP catalogue record for this book is available from
the British Library.

Boxtree takes no responsibility for the use or misuse of apostrophes, bad
spellings or general punctuation abuse throughout this publication.

Designed and typeset by Modern Toss Limited
Printed and bound by Butler and Tanner, Somerset

Visit www.panmacmillan.com to read more about all our books and to buy them. You will
also find features, author interviews and news of any author events, and you can sign up for
e-news letters so that you're always first to hear about our new releases.

MODERN TOSS
ANOTHER BOOK

*from *hitflap*

by Jon Link and Mick Bunnage

B⬛XTREE

high intensity drinking focus group

customer services

that cheap mince i bought off you made me grow a pair of tits

PRINCE EDWARD
~ ROYAL ENTREPRENEUR ~

Gentlemen, welcome to a unique business opportunity, a bag of food hoovered straight out of the mouth of Princess Michael of Kent, whilst she was sleeping in the TV room

Mr Tourette
MASTER SIGNWRITER

can you do a sign for my new bus, I've just sold my flat to pay for it. I need something upbeat to take people's minds off the fact that I've just got out of prison for drink driving

no problem I like a drink myself

Later...

He couldn't even get it out the car park

I could smell it on his fucking breath

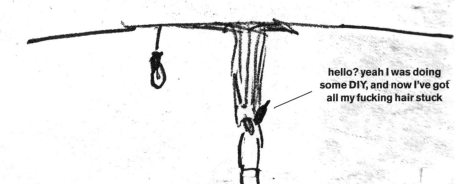

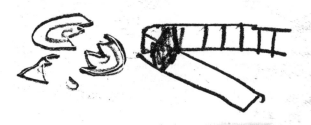

ornamental pigeon breeder

I got this one by making two fat ones have it off and then injecting the egg with a bit of lead, he's called Barry

PARK

I taped a spatula on his back, so it really smears on the pavement

Alan

in "Family Discussion"

Mr Tourette

MASTER SIGNWRITER

I need a sign for my new concept mobile restaurant, I wheel you around a supermarket, you buy the food, then I heat it up in a microwave under the seat. It's for people that live on the go 24-7-365

no problem, that'll look good with a big bit of plywood on top of it

Later...

I've done it on a bendy bit of wire, so when it rains you can flap it over and use it as a roof

... yeah, I'm getting a mixed vibe off it

GARY'S SHITHOLE BUSINESS IDEA

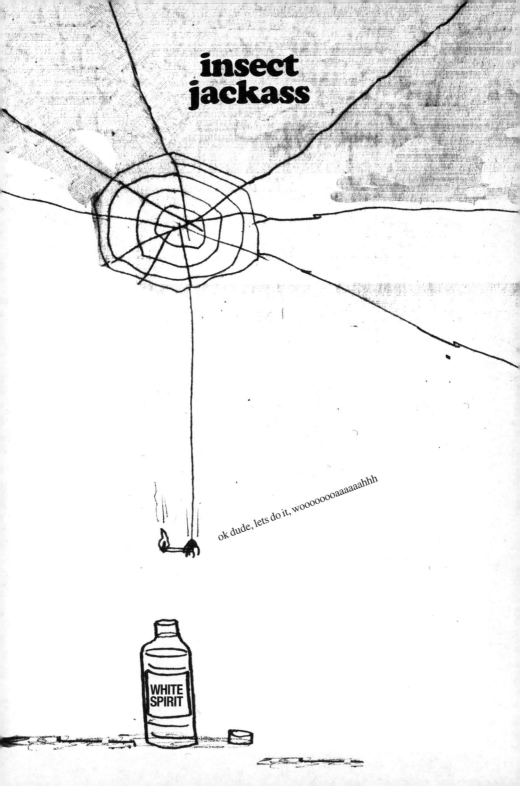

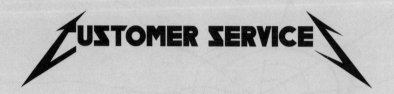

CUSTOMER SERVICES

I came in here yesterday all
pissed up and paid someone to
put a bolt through my cock.
what's your policy on that?

work

daytrippers

at GLYNDEBOURNE

planet chat

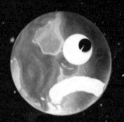

its full on over here, first up I was covered in massive lizards all running around biting each other, next up a load of super evolved apes drilling all me oil out, putting it in cans and burning it

anyone fancy a drink?

i live 'ere

sum man been measuring me field for a mobile ariel mast, he says if it can live in my field he will pay me sum money. sum people from the village come up an are saying no, they say it might get cancer in it. I took one ov em and hung em from the church spire to shut thur noise up

DRIVE-BY ABUSER

that coat makes you look like an arsehole

indoor underwater tv watcher

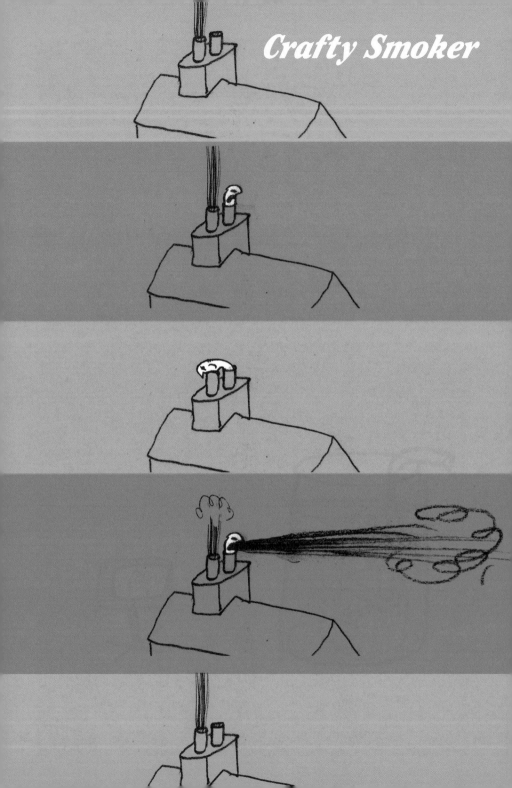

Crafty Smoker

MEDIEVAL KNEVAL
you fucking ready yet or what?
I'm going to catapult myself over a black death pit
alright Medieval, what you up to?

airport security prankster

work

planet chat

sorry about that probe last week, they've got a new space program on the go

yeah, don't worry, heard about the moon? some of them landed on him, took some photos and then fucked off

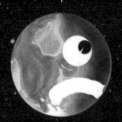

yeah appparently they made a TV programme and a little book out of it, something different innit

Mr Tourette

MASTER SIGNWRITER

Oh hello Mr Tourette, we want to rebrand our funeral shop, we need something contemporary to reflect modern attitudes to "passing on"

yeah, just looking at it makes you feel ill

Later...

oh... Jesus Christ

yeah this should pull some of the younger crowd in, you could franchise it out

Mints Only

but i am fucking mince

no sorry mate, it's mints only

out the way you
plate of guts

Mr Tourette

MASTER SIGNWRITER

Oh hello Mr Tourette can you do me a sign for my Punch and Judy stall. I want something a bit more 'with it'

no problem

Later...

Yeah, I've gone down the heritage route. If you fill in the paperwork I'll send the bill straight to the fucking Arts Council

oh my goodness

work

fly
talk

what happened to you?

I was at this kids party, I'd just
got me tongue round a crisp,
next thing this little kid traps
me in a cup, he shakes it
around so I don't know what
the fuck's going on, then he
rams me torso with a
matchbox car axle...
I don't mind something
different innit

home clubber

PRINCE EDWARD
~ ROYAL ENTREPRENEUR ~

yeah, stuffed a leg on each corner, nailed
a bit of plywood on it and banged the
head on, bloody ingenious... 50 quid each

home clubber

Mr Tourette
MASTER SIGNWRITER

I need a sign for my new chain of coffee shops. I'm calling it "Contemporary Bean Pod" – we'll have ambient world music and Italian sandwiches

are you sure you want to do this, the place is going to fill up with cunts

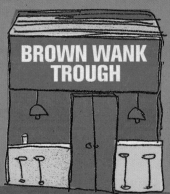

BROWN WANK TROUGH

this is a very ambigious message and you haven't mentioned the sandwiches

£50 quid or I drive my van through the window

MEDIEVAL KNEVAL

LIDO

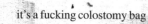

weekend

that robin's in the garden again

have you tried throwing something at it?

♪ PEANUT ♪

HAVING SPENT SOME TIME IN HOSPITAL RECUPERATING, DAVID AND
PAUL OF MOD SUPERGROUP PEANUT GO IN SEARCH OF SOME ANSWERS

DAVID **GARY** **PAUL**

GOOD AFTERNOON GENTLEMEN, CAN I INTEREST YOU IN SOME ORGANICALLY REARED FUCKING FISH? HA HA HA...

SPODSIE!!

I THOUGHT WE MACHINE GUNNED YOUR GUTS OUT

YES THAT'S WHY I'M SAT IN THIS FUCKING WHEELCHAIR, PROJECT MANAGING GARY'S TROUT PORTFOLIO

I'M ALSO PROGRAMMING THE BASS AND DRUMS ON GARY'S NEW ALBUM "FISHNUT", WHAT DO YOU THINK OF THAT THEN?

!?

HOW ABOUT THAT FOR A FUCKING START

BANG

I THOUGHT THAT WENT QUITE WELL... I'M STILL BUZZING

YEAH... I REALLY FEEL LIKE WE'RE STARTING TO GET SOMEWHERE

TO BE CONTINUED

Mr Tourette

MASTER SIGNWRITER

Hello Mr Tourette, can you paint
"Salvation Army Brass Band"
on the bandstand podium?

mmn, ok

Later...

Oh my Christ

Keep your fucking
noise down I'm
trying to relax

DRIVE-BY ABUSER

get a fucking life, yeah

daytrippers

at the Old Bailey

Good idea of yours renting out these judges uniforms we can take over one of the courts and start meting out some proper justice

yeah this cape fits me a treat. I feel like a right tasty cunt. I might smack the gavel into a coppers face on the way in

Nice, I might kick off by flicking piss at the members of the jury, then order them to be hanged

You're well within your rights. I probably won't listen to any of the evidence properly and then just laugh when they read the crimes out

That'll annoy the fuck out of the clerk, you might have to stuff his wig into his fat mouth

Yeah, if I get anyone who hasn't done anything interesting, I might order them to think of something better they could do

Nice one. If I get any of the Royals, I'm going to let them off and then get someone to smack them up later in the car park

Quite right too, I'm dreaming here but if I got Jeff Archer, I'd give him the sword and let him have a swing at some coppers

weekend

did you know that Peter and Jean
are getting divorced?

that should stop them coming round

Alan in "High Rise Meeting"

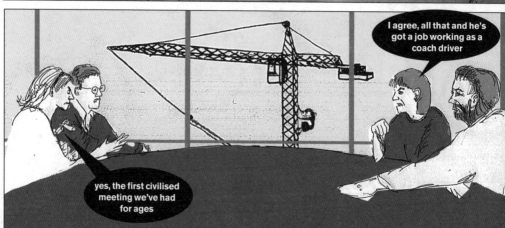

customer services

This DVD player I nicked off you, got me 3 months in prison, where some bloke put his cock in my ear, what are you going to do about it?

ornamental pigeon breeder

I don't know what happened here,
I went on holiday, when I came
back this had happened, he seems
happy enough

customer services

fly
talk

I was up in the back bedroom yeah, flyin' around for about 45 minutes.
I did a full circuit, table lamp, bookcase, then I heard someone coming
up the stairs so I just sat quiet for a bit, he had a look in then fucked off
downstairs again. So I flew down the chimney breast, takes you
straight into the frontroom, went and sat on his flatscreen while he's
trying to watch Quincy, he gets up to swat me and I fly round the back
of him and sick up on his biscuit, then he chases me up the stairs,
whacks his hip on the bannister, now he's seeing a fucking osteopath.

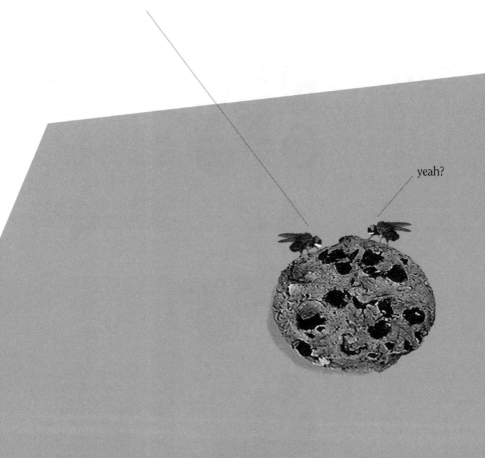

yeah?

daytrippers

in the TOP GEAR audience

homeclubber

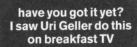

have you got it yet?
I saw Uri Geller do this
on breakfast TV

PRINCE EDWARD
~ ROYAL ENTREPRENEUR ~

points of view

is that the BBC? yeah Titchmarsh came on my telly and I smashed the fuck out of it, I need your details for my insurance company

I WAS
ONLY
TRYING
TO
HELP

health

Hello, have you come for your annual check up?

no i just wondered if you had any change for the crisp machine

customer services

i saw your car advert on the tv where it turns into a robot and goes ice skating, so i went out and bought one, now i want to know where the fucking button is that makes it do that?

Sir Paul Pot
CEO & Chairman

drive-by abuser

work

PEANUT

HAVING EXECUTED THEIR MANAGER SPODSIE FOR THE SECOND TIME, DAVID AND PAUL ARE SEARCHING FOR A NEW FRONT MAN AFTER GARY'S SUCCESSFUL MOVE INTO TROUT FARMING

DAVID   **GARY**   **PAUL**

SUDDENLY

NEVER MIND THAT, GET US A NEW SINGER FOR TOMORROWS GIG OR I'LL RIP YOUR ARM OFF AND WRITE YOUR NAME ON THE WALL WITH IT

WHOA LADS! I'VE ALREADY GOT SOMEONE IN MIND—NOT JUST ANYONE EITHER—THIS BLOKE CAN SING LIKE A FUCKING BIRD

DUNNO SOUNDS A BIT ARTY

THEN...

ALRIGHT, YOU'VE GOT TILL MIDNIGHT TO DELIVER AND HE BETTER NOT BE SOME **BONGO FUCK-UP MERCHANT!**

YEAH OR YOU'LL SPEND THE REST OF YOUR LIFE LIVING IN A COFFIN UNDERGROUND

ALRIGHT LADS LEAVE IT WITH ME

...ATER...

RIGHT! WHAT SORT OF MUSIC DO YOU LIKE?

...I LIKE BONGO MUSIC

NO YOU FUCKIN DON'T ...HAVE ANOTHER GO!

health

how much to graft these onto my wife

tv showroom

I just coughed up all over this flatscreen, how does that affect the price?

fly talk

we've been hanging round at Paul McCartney's place, thought i was listening to some new material but then i realised he was just singing 'fucking slag' to the tune of Michelle

yeah I think we're all going to get a bit of a shock when the new album comes out, I've had a look at the artwork, it's basically him with his thumbs up as per usual but he's got her severed head on a table in front of him

whats he been pissing about on the old photoshop has he?

work

SPACE ARGUMENT

When a child is born

customer services

I pissed myself on your floor, then i slipped in it
and ended up as a fucking paraplegic get your cheque book out

work

I'm thinking about leaving, do you want to have a whip round for my present and I'll see if it's worth it

i live 'ere

sum bloke cum to me
ouse, he wonts to sell me
a wire with a braidband
running thru it to connect
to a web. he showed me a
book with pictures
of people watchun a
white telly and robot type-
writers. as he was
leaving i shot him in the
back , now e's
sitting in me shed   wiv
a potato grown out of his
mouf

BUFFALO BUILDER

home~clubber

daytrippers

at a Will Young record signing

W hat's going on today?

Will Young is signing copies of his new single in Woolworths

that sounds well shit, and why you got me sat on this disability cart?

this will get us access to the front of the queue where
I'm going to wedge his big fat old chin in the basket

I'll get his stinking little feet trapped in my basket

yeah then we can go backwards and forwards and stretch the
fucker till he looks like a pipecleaner with a chin on top

do you reckon that's the sort of publicity he's looking for?

yeah I reckon his PR Machine will be well chuffed with that

Mr Tourette

MASTER SIGNWRITER

crafty smoker

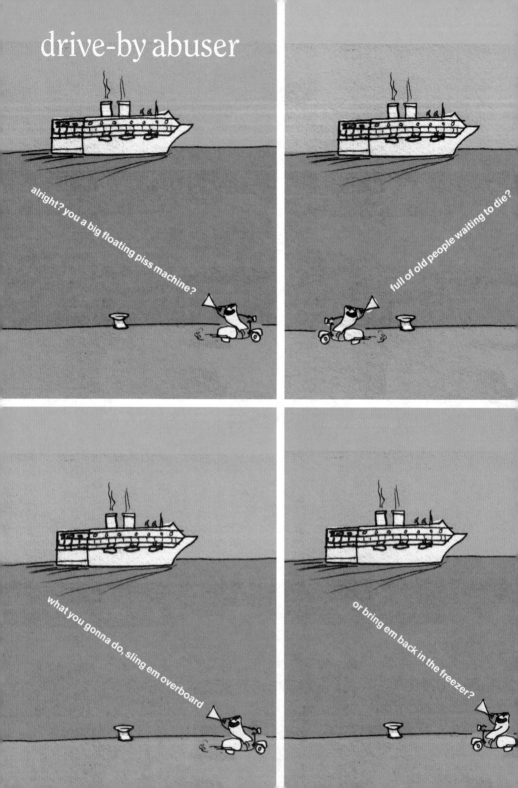

home~clubber

I've been researching my family tree on the internet, so far all I've found is a photo of my sister naked with a lorry driver

When
a child is
born

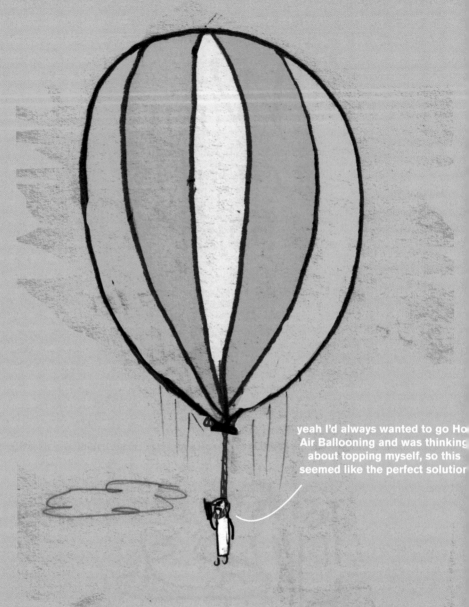

yeah I'd always wanted to go Ho
Air Ballooning and was thinking
about topping myself, so this
seemed like the perfect solution

*extreme
leisure
time*

Dogkiller

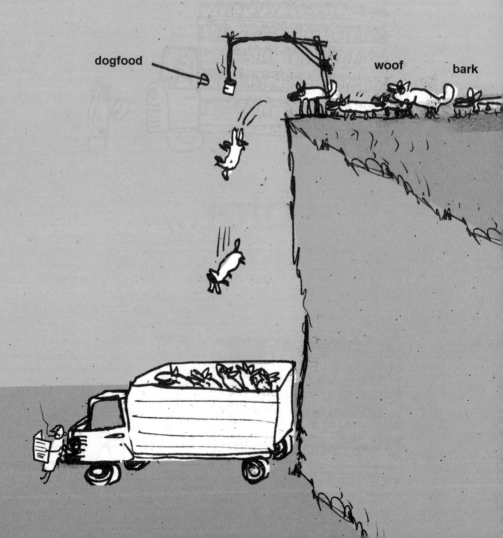

fly talk

I spotted that James Blunt the other day,
he's in disguise and that so
I followed him into a record shop and he
starts watching people as they're looking
at his cds, he's taking pictures of them
with his mobile, obviously planning on a
long stint because he's got some
sandwiches with him, then a security
guard spots him so he tries to make a run
for it, knocks himself out on a glass door,
then the Police turned up, took his
autograph and let him go...

fucking embarrassing innit

Alan

in "the Beach Hut"

LATER...

Mr Tourette
MASTER SIGNWRITER

Sir Paul Pot
CEO & Chairman

999

Get a pump round here I've eaten 2 litre tubs of Belgian chocolate, normally I just chuck it up.

daytrippers

at the Winter Gardens X Factor concert

what's going on with this
Winter Gardens thing then?

yeah it's the X factor
lot singing the hits of
Cole Porter

that sounds a bit boring,
I wouldn't have thought
that'ud be your sort of thing

it's not, as soon as the first
fucker opens his mouth to sing
I'm going to stuff this tree
stump in his mouth

what's your thinking
behind that then?

when it's in his mouth I'm
going to twist it round and
sharpen it on his teeth

so you are in fact using his face
like a human tree sharpener?
do you reckon that'll stop him
singing then?

don't suppose he'll want to
carry on after that, meanwhile
I'll be using the sharpened
stick to battle our way out
through security

home~clubber

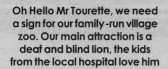

Mr Tourette
MASTER SIGNWRITER

Oh Hello Mr Tourette, we need a sign for our family-run village zoo. Our main attraction is a deaf and blind lion, the kids from the local hospital love him

yeah I wondered what the fucking smell was

Later...

fuck me

ANIMAL STINK PRISON

I hope you're insured. One of the monkeys started flinging his shit about and I might have swallowed a bit

BUFFALO BUILDER

cheese&wine

just been to the toilet, it's a bit dark up there, think I might have pissed all over the coats

home~clubber

I've got a new job doing air traffic control, but I insisted on working from home. Do you want a go? I got a big'un coming in

customer services

daytrippers

on a Historic Walk

What times the coach go back then?

it's picking us up from the other end of this historic walk

what's the guide book say?

it says there's a ruined abbey on the way

already ruined? what they bring us here for then

well there's a big lump of it still up, I'm going to knock it down and concrete it over

that'll be handy you can cross it straight out the guidebook

ok let's get going, it's not going to shit itself up is it?

drive-by abuser

what are you grinning at you cunt?

weekend

Sir Paul Pot

CEO & Chairman

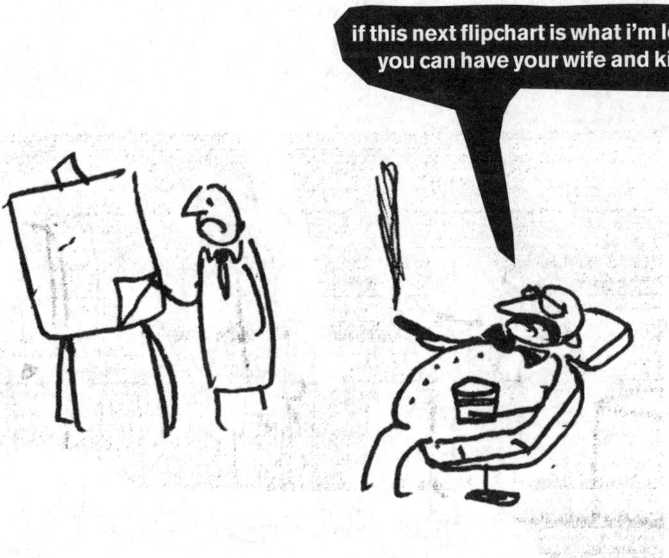